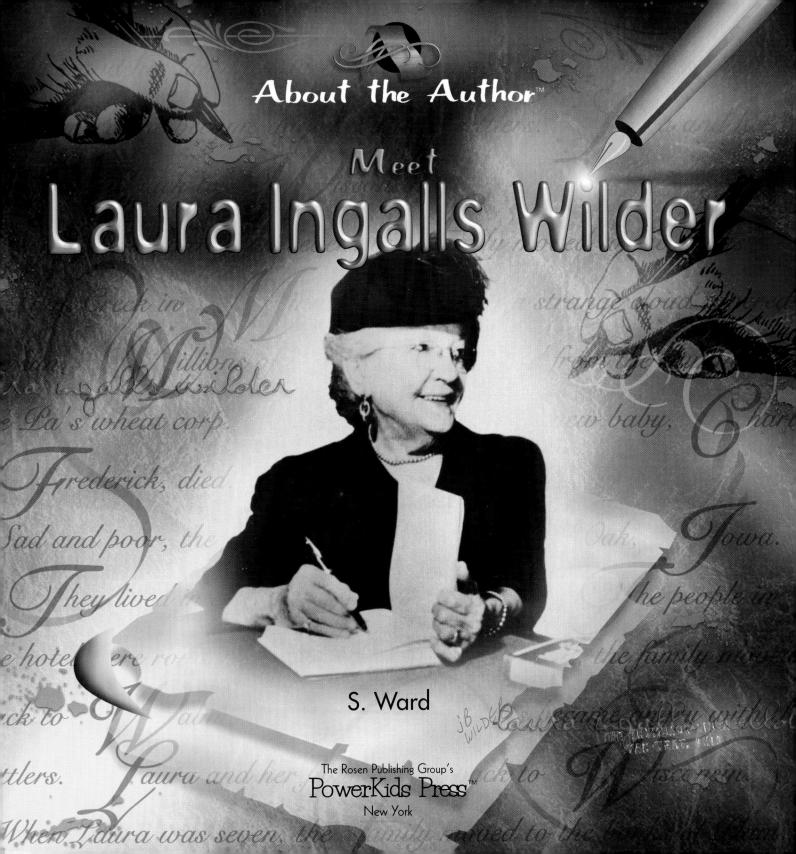

About the Author™

Meet

Laura Ingalls Wilder

S. Ward

The Rosen Publishing Group's
PowerKids Press™
New York

Published in 2001 by The Rosen Publishing Group, Inc.
29 East 21st Street, New York, NY 10010

First Edition

Book Design: Maria Melendez

Photo Credits: Cover, title page © The Everett Collection; pp. 3, 4, 6, 7, 12, 15, 16, 17, 18, 19, 21, 23 © Courtesy of Laura Ingalls Wilder Home Association; pp. 11, 14 © Courtesy of Laura Ingalls Wilder Memorial Society.

Grateful acknowledgment is made for permission to reprint previously published material on pp. 5, 8, 10, and 20: from LITTLE HOUSE IN THE BIG WOODS by Laura Ingalls Wilder, text copyright 1932 by Laura Ingalls Wilder, text copyright renewed 1959, 1987 by Roger Lea MacBride, illustrations copyright 1953 by Garth Williams, illustrations copyright renewed 1981 by Garth Williams, first published in 1932, revised edition, illustrated by Garth Williams, published in 1953, first Harper Trophy edition, 1971; ON THE BANKS OF PLUM CREEK by Laura Ingalls Wilder, illustrated by Garth Williams, text copyright 1937 by Laura Ingalls Wilder, text copyright renewed 1965, 1993 by Roger Lea MacBride, illustrations copyright 1953 by Garth Williams, illustrations copyright renewed 1981 by Garth Williams, first published in 1937, revised edition, illustrated by Garth Williams, published in 1953, first Harper Trophy edition, 1971; BY THE SHORES OF SILVER LAKE, by Laura Ingalls Wilder, text copyright 1939 by Laura Ingalls Wilder, text copyright renewed 1967 by Roger Lea MacBride, illustrations copyright 1953 by Garth Williams, illustrations copyright renewed 1981 by Garth Williams, first published in 1939, revised edition, illustrated by Garth Williams, published in 1953, first Harper Trophy edition, 1971; LITTLE HOUSE ON THE PRAIRIE by Laura Ingalls Wilder, text copyright 1935 by Laura Ingalls Wilder, text copyright renewed 1963 by Roger Lea MacBride, illustrations copyright 1953 by Garth Williams, illustrations copyright renewed 1981 by Garth Williams, first published in 1935, revised edition, illustrated by Garth Williams, published in 1953, first Harper Trophy edition, 1971; published by arrangement with HarperCollins Children's Books, a division of HarperCollins Publishers, Inc., and used with permission by HarperCollins Publishers, Inc.

Ward, S.
    Meet Laura Ingalls Wilder / S. Ward.—1st ed.
      p. cm. — (About the author)
    Includes index.
    Summary: A brief biography of the well-known author of the "Little House" books, which tell the story of the writer's family life and experiences growing up on the frontier.
    ISBN 0-8239-5712-8 (alk. paper)
      1. Wilder, Laura Ingalls, 1867–1957—Juvenile literature. 2. Authors, American—20th century—Biography—Juvenile literature. 3. Frontier and pioneer life—United States—Juvenile literature. 4. Children's stories—Authorship—Juvenile literature. [1. Wilder, Laura Ingalls, 1867–1957. 2. Authors, American. 3. Women—Biography.] I. Title. II. Series.
    PS3545.I342 Z94 2000
    813'.52—dc21
    [B]
                                                                            00-025374

Manufactured in the United States of America

Contents

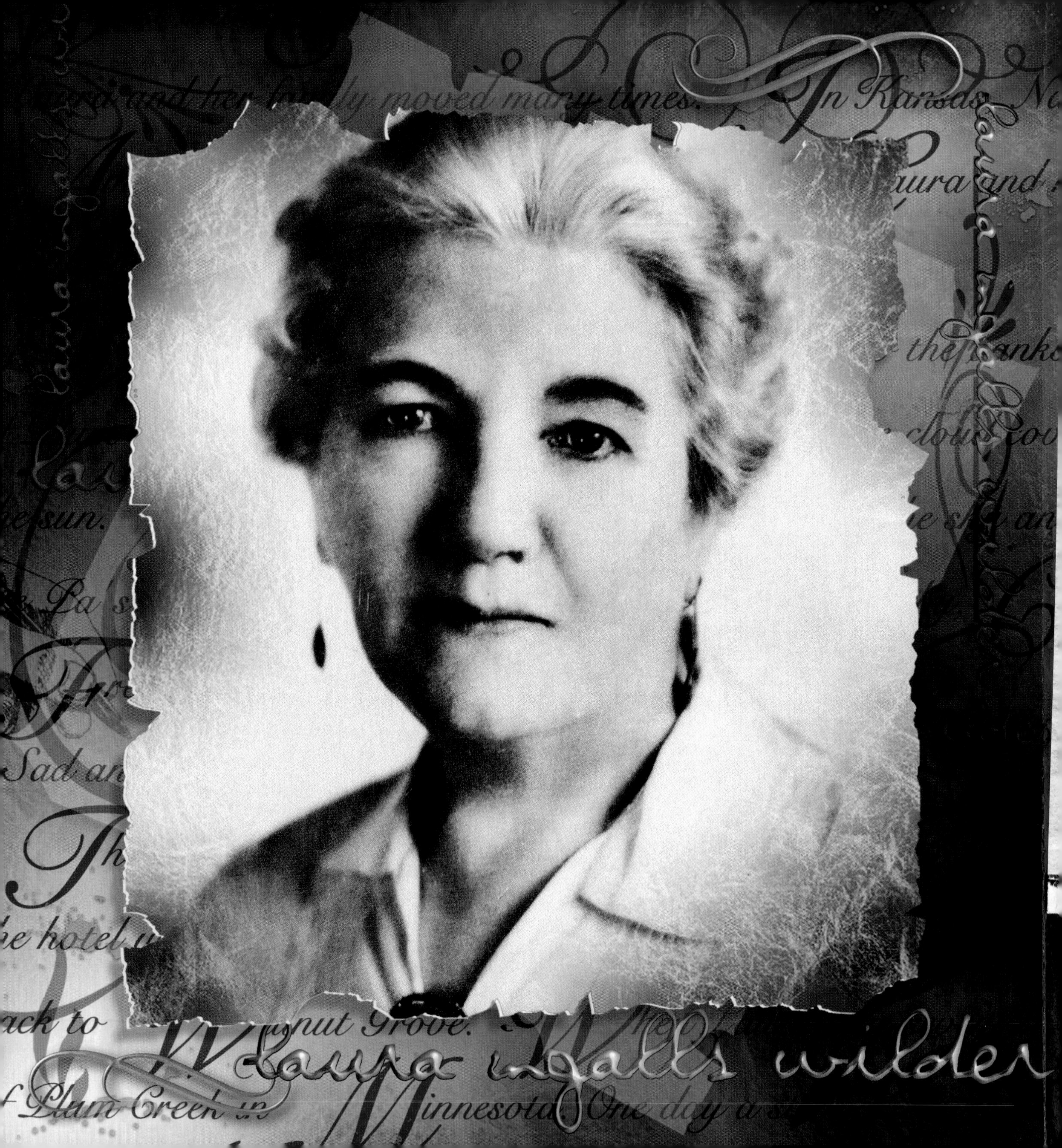
laura ingalls wilder

Little House in the Big Woods

In 1930, on a farm near Mansfield, Missouri, a woman began to write a story. The story was about her **childhood** in the Wisconsin woods. The woman was 63 years old when she wrote the story. Her name was Laura Ingalls Wilder.

Harper and Brothers **publishing company** bought Laura's story to make it into a book. *Little House in the Big Woods* was published in April 1932. The book was a success. It got great **reviews** and won awards. Readers wrote to Laura to ask for more stories. She wrote more books about her childhood. The little house where she had lived soon became world famous.

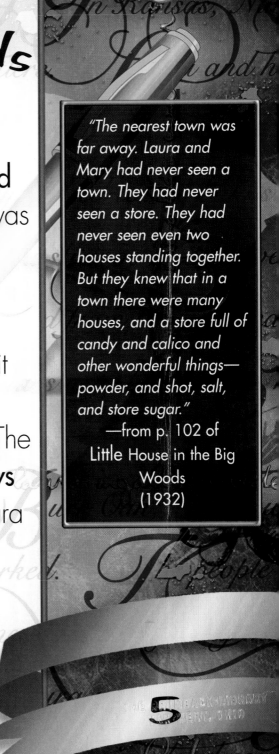

"The nearest town was far away. Laura and Mary had never seen a town. They had never seen a store. They had never seen even two houses standing together. But they knew that in a town there were many houses, and a store full of candy and calico and other wonderful things— powder, and shot, salt, and store sugar."
—from p. 102 of
Little House in the Big Woods
(1932)

◀ *This photograph of Laura Ingalls Wilder was taken in 1937.*

From the Woods to the Prairies

Laura Elizabeth Ingalls was born near Pepin, Wisconsin, on February 7, 1867. Her parents' names were Charles and Caroline. Her big sister's name was Mary. Laura called her parents Pa and Ma. She wished she had golden hair like her sister. Laura's hair was brown, and she thought it was too plain.

The family lived in a little log cabin in the woods of Wisconsin. Ma liked their home but Pa wanted to go farther west. When Laura was three, Pa packed the family into a covered wagon. In 1870, they moved to the **prairies** of Kansas. Laura's little sister Carrie was born while the family lived in Kansas.

Caroline and Charles Ingalls were married in 1860. The Ingalls family lived far away from most people. They had to learn to do many things for themselves.

Laura and her family moved many times.
laura ingalls wilder
When Laura was seven, the
Plum Creek in Minnesota. One day a st

and her family moved many times.
In Kansas
laura ingalls wilder
innesota. One day a

Many Moves

The Ingalls family moved many times. In Kansas, Native Americans became angry with settlers, like the Ingalls, for taking their land. Laura and her family had a difficult time settling in Kansas and in time moved back to Wisconsin.

When Laura was seven, the family moved to a **dugout house** near Plum Creek in Walnut Grove, Minnesota. One day a strange cloud covered the sun. The cloud was millions of grasshoppers. They dropped from the sky and ate Pa's wheat crop. Then in 1876, Pa and Ma's baby son, Charles Frederic, died. Sad and poor, the family then moved to Burr Oak, Iowa.

This illustration is from Laura's book On the ◀ Banks of Plum Creek. *It shows the Ingalls family arriving at their dugout house.*

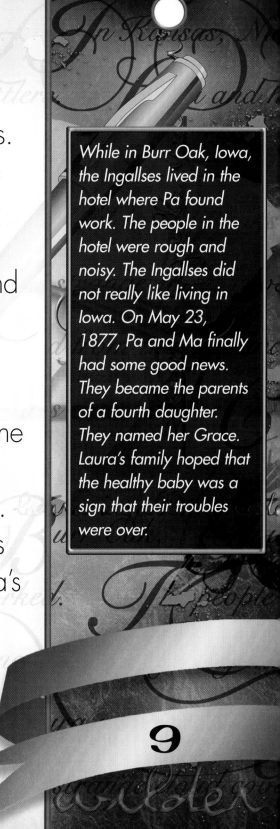

While in Burr Oak, Iowa, the Ingallses lived in the hotel where Pa found work. The people in the hotel were rough and noisy. The Ingallses did not really like living in Iowa. On May 23, 1877, Pa and Ma finally had some good news. They became the parents of a fourth daughter. They named her Grace. Laura's family hoped that the healthy baby was a sign that their troubles were over.

Mary's Eyes

In the fall of 1877, the family returned to Walnut Grove. Laura and Mary went to school. They were happy to be studying with their old friends. Laura enjoyed Friday night spelling bees. She also liked to have snowball fights and play baseball. Mary was more ladylike. She wanted to study and become a teacher like Ma.

Then Mary got very sick. Doctors said she had "brain fever," or **meningitis**. The sickness left Mary blind. Laura promised Pa that she would become "Mary's eyes." She would describe everything she saw to Mary.

Laura and two of her sisters, from left to right: Carrie, Laura, and Mary. Laura wanted to become a teacher after Mary became blind. ▶

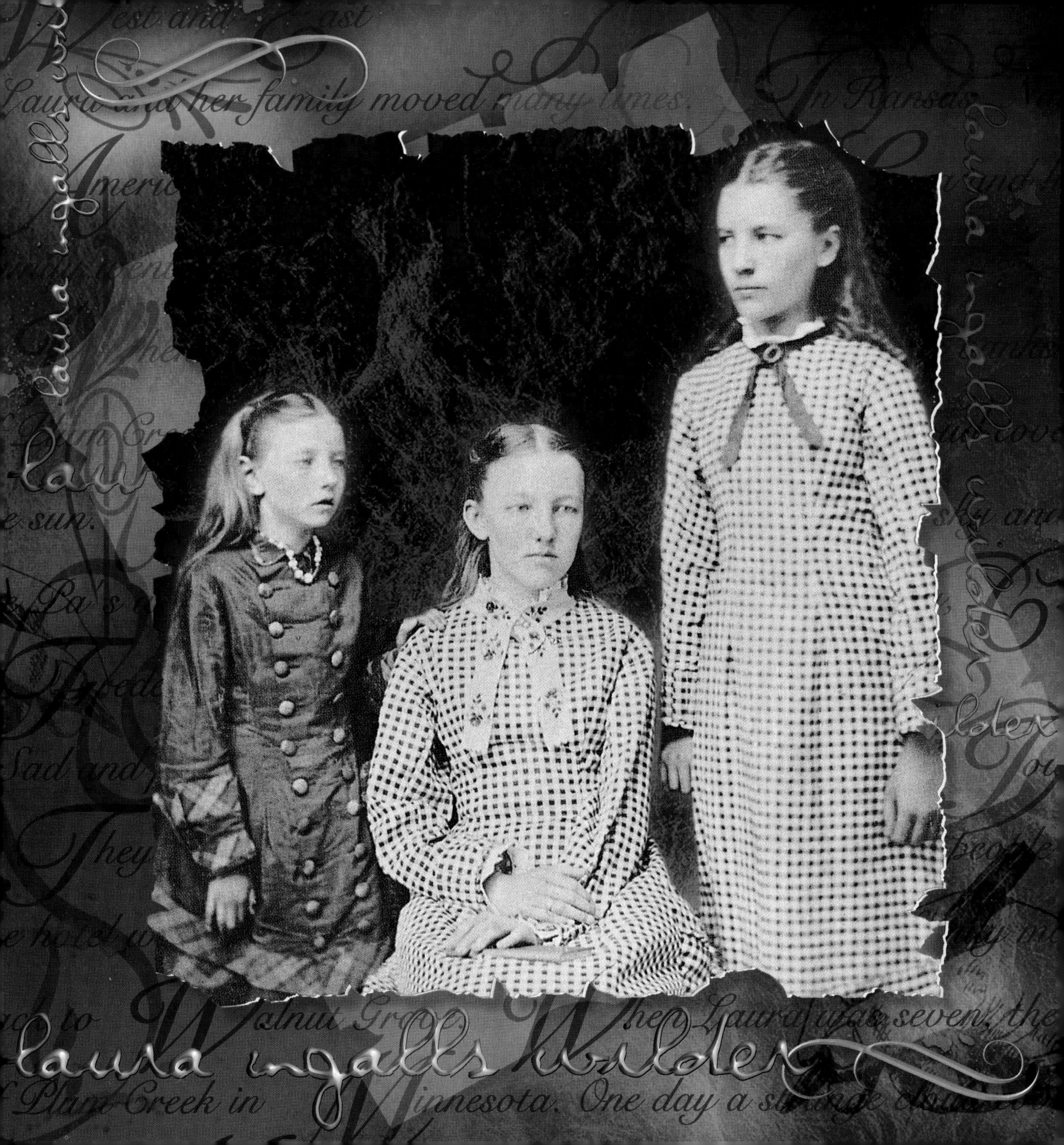

Dakota Territory

Soon Pa went west again. This time he went to work for the railroad. When Mary was well enough, Ma and the girls boarded a train to join Pa in the town of De Smet in Dakota Territory. Dakota Territory included today's states of Wyoming, Montana, North Dakota, and South Dakota. On the train, Laura told Mary about all the places that they passed through on their way to De Smet. The family made a new home along Silver Lake. There was plenty of food. Pa played the fiddle at night. His music-playing helped cheer them in good times and bad. Ma read stories from the newspaper. The fall was a happy time for the Ingalls family.

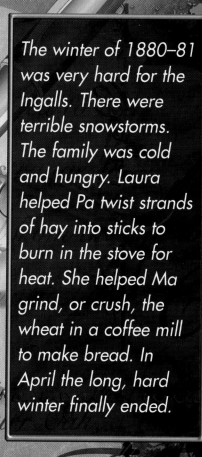

The winter of 1880–81 was very hard for the Ingalls. There were terrible snowstorms. The family was cold and hungry. Laura helped Pa twist strands of hay into sticks to burn in the stove for heat. She helped Ma grind, or crush, the wheat in a coffee mill to make bread. In April the long, hard winter finally ended.

◀ *Laura's father played this fiddle. Laura wrote about Pa's music-playing in many of her books, including* Little House on the Prairie.

13

Almanzo and Rose

Laura worked to help pay for Mary's schooling at the School for the Blind in Vinton, Iowa. In 1883, Laura got a teaching job. She lived with a family near the school. She wanted to be with her own family. A farmer named Almanzo Wilder came to drive her home to see her family. Almanzo and Laura fell in love. They got married on August 25, 1885. They settled on a farm north of De Smet. In December 1886, Laura and Almanzo had a baby daughter, Rose. They were happy about the baby but were sad about many other things. **Drought** and **hail** ruined their crops. Almanzo got sick, and then the house burned down.

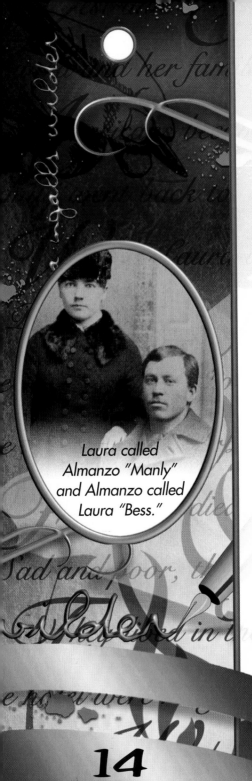

Laura called Almanzo "Manly" and Almanzo called Laura "Bess."

Laura and Almanzo's baby daughter, Rose, was born on December 5, 1886. Rose would grow up to be a well-known writer.

Laura and her family moved many times. In Florida

to Walnut Grove. When Laura was seven, the

Plum Creek in Minnesota. One day a strange

laura ingalls wilder

Farmer and Writer

In 1894, Laura, Almanzo, and their daughter, Rose, moved to Mansfield, Missouri. They bought land and built a home that they called Rocky Ridge Farm. Laura loved Rocky Ridge Farm. She raised chickens there. Almanzo raised horses. Laura and Almanzo worked together to care for the cows and apple trees. Laura also worked for the Farm Loan Association. She helped farmers get money to plant crops. She was very busy and happy.

Rose grew up and moved to California. She became a well-known writer. Laura began to write, too. She wrote about being a farmer's wife.

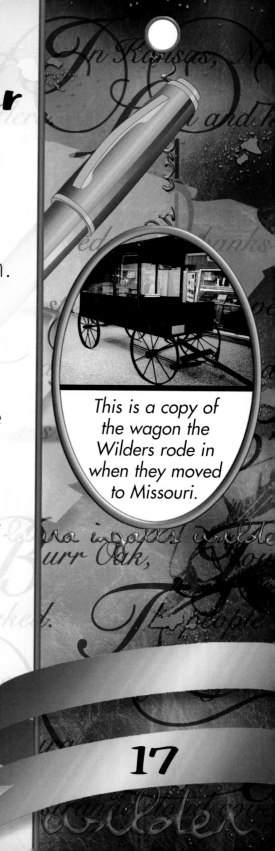

This is a copy of the wagon the Wilders rode in when they moved to Missouri.

◀ *Today Rocky Ridge Farm is known as the Laura Ingalls Wilder Home and Museum.*

Stories From Childhood

By the 1930s, Laura was getting older. Pa, Ma, and Mary had already died. Laura worried that no one would remember the stories Pa had told her as a young girl. People were forgetting about the way life had been before there had been cars and electric lights. She decided to write her **autobiography**. She described her life from her childhood to her marriage to Almanzo. She gave the story to her daughter, Rose. Rose typed the story. She also helped her mother make it sound better. Laura turned the story into a book about her girlhood in Wisconsin. *Little House in the Big Woods* was printed in 1932.

Laura wrote about this jewel box in On the Banks of Plum Creek.

This is Laura's study in her home on Rocky Ridge Farm. She wrote her books at this desk. She wrote in pencil in a blue-lined school notebook. ▶

Laura and her family moved many times.
laura ingalls wilder
Plum Creek in Minnesota. One day a strange
When Laura was seven, the

LAURA INGALLS WILDER

Little House on the Prairie

Illustrated by Garth Williams

LITTLE HOUSE ON THE PRAIRIE
65TH Anniversary

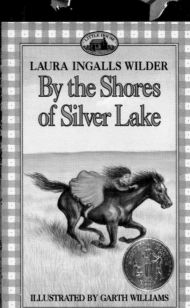

LAURA INGALLS WILDER

By the Shores of Silver Lake

Illustrated by Garth Williams

LAURA INGALLS WILDER

On the Banks of Plum Creek

Illustrated by Garth Williams

The "Little House" Books

Laura wrote six more books about her childhood and one book about Almanzo's. Readers loved her stories and wrote letters to her. Laura answered a lot of these letters.

On October 23, 1949, Almanzo died. Laura said she did not feel like writing anymore. Secretly, though, she wrote another book about the first four years of being married to Almanzo. Laura put the book in a drawer and did not show it to anyone.

Laura was given many honors. Libraries were named after her. A special writer's award was named after her in 1954. Laura died on February 10, 1957.

In many of her books, Laura retold some of Pa's favorite stories. Laura wrote about things she remembered. She changed a few things to make the stories work better.

Laura's mailbox was often full of fan letters.

A New Century of Readers

After Laura died, her daughter, Rose, found one of her mother's notebooks. In it Laura had written about moving to Mansfield. Rose added some of her own stories to make a book called *On the Way Home*. Rose died in 1968. Soon after, Rose's adopted grandson, Roger MacBride, found Laura's secret story about her early years with Almanzo. He had the book published with the title *The First Four Years* in 1971. The events Laura wrote about took place more than 100 years ago. Today her books seem more interesting than ever. Laura was right. Her life was well worth remembering.

These objects traveled with Laura and Almanzo from Dakota Territory to Missouri.

Glossary

autobiography (aw-toh-by-AH-gruh-fee) A story written about one's own life.

childhood (CHYLD-hood) The time of life between being a baby and being a teenager.

drought (DROWT) A long period of dry weather with little or no rain.

dugout house (DUG-owt HOWS) A type of house dug into the ground or the side of a hill.

hail (HAYL) Small pieces of ice that sometimes fall during a thunderstorm.

meningitis (meh-nin-JY-tis) A type of illness in which a bacterial infection can cause an inflammation of the brain and the spinal cord. It can be deadly if it is not treated early.

prairies (PRAYR-ees) Large areas of flat land with grass but few or no trees.

publishing company (PUH-blish-ing KUM-puh-nee) A business that prints things, such as books or magazines, for people to read.

reviews (rih-VYOOZ) Opinions about a performance or book.

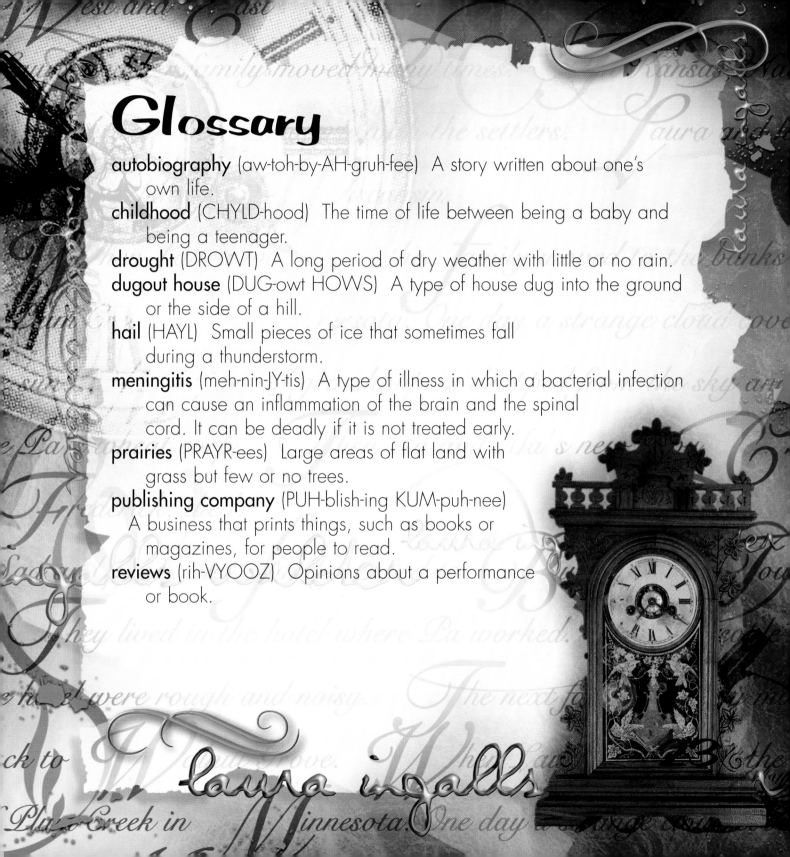

Index

Web Sites

To learn more about Laura Ingalls Wilder, check out these Web Sites:

http://www.bestoftheozarks.com/wilderhome (The Laura Ingalls Wilder Home and Museum)

http://www.vvv.com/~jenslegg/ (My Little House on the Prairie Home Page of Laura Ingalls Wilder)